100 INSPIRATIONAL QUOTES BY ALBERT CAMUS

QANA BOOKS

OTHER INSPIRATIONAL BOOKS IN THE SERIES:

100 Inspirational Quotes by Mark Twain
100 Inspirational Quotes by Mahatma Gandhi
100 Inspirational Quotes by Oscar Wilde
100 Inspirational Quotes by Friedrich Nietzsche
100 Inspirational Quotes by Confucius
100 Inspirational Quotes by Aristotle
100 Inspirational Quotes by Malcom X
100 Inspirational Quotes by Gautama Buddha
100 Inspirational Quotes by Ali ibn Abi Talib
100 Inspirational Quotes by Winston Churchill
100 Inspirational Quotes by Plato
100 Inspirational Quotes by **Bertrand Russell**

Collection copyright © 2022 Qana Books

All rights reserved

Cover design by Saracen Studios

ISBN: 9798359852050

ALBERT CAMUS

Albert Camus was a 20th century French philosopher, author and journalist. He was awarded the Nobel Prize in Literature in 1957 at the age of 44, making him the second-youngest recipient in its history.

Camus was born in French Algeria and studied philosophy at the University of Algiers. He was part of the French Resistance in the Second World War where he served as editor-in-chief at Combat, an outlawed newspaper.

Philosophically, Camus's views contributed to the rise of the philosophy known as Absurdism. Some consider Camus's work to show him to be an existentialist, even though he himself firmly rejected the term throughout his lifetime.

100 Inspirational Quotes by Albert Camus

The only way to deal with an unfree world is to become so absolutely free that your very existence is an act of rebellion

100 Inspirational Quotes by Albert Camus

Men must live and create. Live to the point of tears

Nobody realizes that some people expend tremendous energy merely to be normal

Those who lack the courage will always find a philosophy to justify it

Nothing is more despicable than respect based on fear

100 Inspirational Quotes by Albert Camus

Real generosity toward the future lies in giving all to the present

To be happy we must not be too concerned with others

No cause justifies the deaths of innocent people

100 Inspirational Quotes by Albert Camus

Alas, after a certain age every man is responsible for his face

Truth, like light, blinds. Falsehood, on the contrary, is a beautiful twilight that enhances every object

By definition, a government has no conscience. Sometimes it has a policy, but nothing more

The modern mind is in complete disarray. Knowledge has stretched itself to the point where neither the world nor our intelligence can find any foothold. It is a fact that we are suffering from nihilism

Without freedom, no art; art lives only on the restraints it imposes on itself, and dies of all others

The absurd is the essential concept and the first truth

Basically, at the very bottom of life, which seduces us all, there is only absurdity, and more absurdity. And maybe that's what gives us our joy for living, because the only thing that can defeat absurdity is lucidity

Autumn is a second spring when every leaf is a flower

A man's work is nothing but this slow trek to rediscover, through the detours of art, those two or three great and simple images in whose presence his heart first opened

Blessed are the hearts that can bend; they shall never be broken

In the depth of winter I finally learned that there was in me an invincible summer

Every act of rebellion expresses a nostalgia for innocence and an appeal to the essence of being

The only real progress lies in learning to be wrong all alone

To know oneself, one should assert oneself

Integrity has no need of rules

He who despairs of the human condition is a coward, but he who has hope for it is a fool

A free press can, of course, be good or bad, but, most certainly without freedom, the press will never be anything but bad

Without work, all life goes rotten. But when work is soulless, life stifles and dies

Some people talk in their sleep. Lecturers talk while other people sleep

As a remedy to life in society I would suggest the big city. Nowadays, it is the only desert within our means

I would rather live my life as if there is a God and die to find out there isn't, than live as if there isn't and to die to find out that there is

A man without ethics is a wild beast loosed upon this world

Beauty is unbearable, drives us to despair, offering us for a minute the glimpse of an eternity that we should like to stretch out over the whole of time

The struggle itself towards the heights is enough to fill a man's heart. One must imagine Sisyphus happy

Freedom is nothing but a chance to be better

Man is the only creature that refuses to be what he is

The welfare of the people in particular has always been the alibi of tyrants

We continue to shape our personality all our life. If we knew ourselves perfectly, we should die

In order to exist, man must rebel, but rebellion must respect the limits that it discovers in itself - limits where minds meet, and in meeting, begin to exist

I know of only one duty, and that is to love

In order to understand the world, one has to turn away from it on occasion

Charm is a way of getting the answer 'Yes' without asking a clear question

100 Inspirational Quotes by Albert Camus

Heroism is accessible. Happiness is more difficult

Friendship often ends in love, but love in friendship - never

Stupidity has a knack of getting its way

You will never be happy if you continue to search for what happiness consists of. You will never live if you are looking for the meaning of life

Without culture, and the relative freedom it implies, society, even when perfect, is but a jungle. This is why any authentic creation is a gift to the future

You cannot create experience. You must undergo it

All great deeds and all great thoughts have a ridiculous beginning. Great works are often born on a street corner or in a restaurant's revolving door

But what is happiness except the simple harmony between a man and the life he leads

There is no love of life without despair of life

The world is never quiet, even its silence eternally resounds with the same notes, in vibrations which escape our ears. As for those that we perceive, they carry sounds to us, occasionally a chord, never a melody

The need to be right is the sign of a vulgar mind

The evil that is in the world almost always comes of ignorance, and good intentions may do as much harm as malevolence if they lack understanding

We always deceive ourselves twice about the people we love - first to their advantage, then to their disadvantage

Truth is mysterious, elusive, always to be conquered. Liberty is dangerous, as hard to live with as it is elating. We must march toward these two goals, painfully but resolutely, certain in advance of our failings on so long a road

100 Inspirational Quotes by Albert Camus

It is not your paintings I like, it is your painting

It is necessary to fall in love... if only to provide an alibi for all the random despair you are going to feel anyway

There is no fate that cannot be surmounted by scorn

Don't wait for the last judgment - it takes place every day

We get into the habit of living before acquiring the habit of thinking. In that race which daily hastens us towards death, the body maintains its irreparable lead

What is a rebel? A man who says no: but whose refusal does not imply a renunciation

It is a kind of spiritual snobbery that makes people think they can be happy without money

At 30 a man should know himself like the palm of his hand, know the exact number of his defects and qualities, know how far he can go, foretell his failures - be what he is. And, above all, accept these things

There is in me an anarchy and frightful disorder. Creating makes me die a thousand deaths, because it means making order, and my entire being rebels against order. But without it I would die, scattered to the winds

I should like to be able to love my country and still love justice

A taste for truth at any cost is a passion which spares nothing

Lying is not only saying what isn't true. It is also, in fact especially, saying more than is true and, in the case of the human heart, saying more than one feels. We all do it, every day, to make life simpler

Every great work makes the human face more admirable and richer, and that is its whole secret

Those who weep for the happy periods which they encounter in history acknowledge what they want; not the alleviation but the silencing of misery

Your successes and happiness are forgiven you only if you generously consent to share them

An intellectual is someone whose mind watches itself

Men are convinced of your arguments, your sincerity, and the seriousness of your efforts only by your death

Too many have dispensed with generosity in order to practice charity

Real nobility is based on scorn, courage, and profound indifference

A guilty conscience needs to confess.
A work of art is a confession

Truly fertile Music, the only kind that will move us, that we shall truly appreciate, will be a Music conducive to Dream, which banishes all reason and analysis. One must not wish first to understand and then to feel. Art does not tolerate Reason

No matter what cause one defends, it will suffer permanent disgrace if one resorts to blind attacks on crowds of innocent people

100 Inspirational Quotes by Albert Camus

Culture: the cry of men in face of their destiny

Don't believe your friends when they ask you to be honest with them. All they really want is to be maintained in the good opinion they have of themselves

Man wants to live, but it is useless to hope that this desire will dictate all his actions

Against eternal injustice, man must assert justice, and to protest against the universe of grief, he must create happiness

Virtue cannot separate itself from reality without becoming a principle of evil

The society based on production is only productive, not creative

There is the good and the bad, the great and the low, the just and the unjust. I swear to you that all that will never change

Those who write clearly have readers, those who write obscurely have commentators

The role of the intellectual cannot be to excuse the violence of one side and condemn that of the other

We rarely confide in those who are better than we are

It is normal to give away a little of one's life in order not to lose it all

How can sincerity be a condition of friendship? A taste for truth at any cost is a passion which spares nothing

Rebellion cannot exist without the feeling that somewhere, in some way, you are justified

After all manner of professors have done their best for us, the place we are to get knowledge is in books. The true university of these days is a collection of books

100 Inspirational Quotes by Albert Camus

Violence is both unavoidable and unjustifiable

Every artist preserves deep within him a single source from which, throughout his lifetime, he draws what he is, and what he says. When the source dries up, the work withers and crumbles

You have to be very rich or very poor to live without a trade

Working conditions for me have always been those of the monastic life: solitude and frugality. Except for frugality, they are contrary to my nature, so much so that work is a violence I do to myself

Methods of thought which claim to give the lead to our world in the name of revolution have become, in reality, ideologies of consent and not of rebellion

To assert in any case that a man must be absolutely cut off from society because he is absolutely evil amounts to saying that society is absolutely good, and no-one in his right mind will believe this today

100 Inspirational Quotes by Albert Camus

We call first truths those we discover after all the others

100 Inspirational Quotes by Albert Camus

The day when I am no more than a writer I shall cease to be a writer

Retaliation is related to nature and instinct, not to law. Law, by definition, cannot obey the same rules as nature

The absurd depends as much on man as on the world. For the moment, it is all that links them together

Printed in Great Britain
by Amazon